castings

MANDY HAGGITH

TWO RAVENS PRESS

Published by Two Ravens Press
Green Willow Croft
Rhiroy
Loch Broom
Ullapool
Ross-shire IV23 2SF

www.tworavenspress.com

ISBN: 978-1-906120-01-6

British Library Cataloguing in Publication Data. A CIP record
for this book can be obtained from the British Library.

Designed and typeset by Two Ravens Press
Cover design by David Knowles and Sharon Blackie

Printed on Forest Stewardship Council-accredited paper by
Biddles Ltd., King's Lynn, Norfolk.

About the Author

Mandy Haggith first studied Philosophy and Mathematics and then Artificial Intelligence, and spent years struggling to write elegant computer programs that could help to save the planet. A decade ago she left academia to pursue a life of writing and revolution, and has since travelled all over the world researching forests and the people dependent on them, and campaigning for their protection. In 2003, she returned to Glasgow University to study for an MPhil in Creative Writing, gaining a distinction. This is her first book-length collection of poetry, though a pamphlet, *letting light in*, was published in 2005. She lives on a woodland croft in Assynt, in the Scottish Highlands.

Acknowledgements

I would like to thank Glasgow University's Creative Writers, particularly Tom Leonard, for insightful criticism and encouragement; the Northwest Highlands Writers for their camaraderie; David and Sharon at Two Ravens Press for being textually and environmentally sensitive; the Scottish Arts Council for funding a winter of writing; and Bill for supporting me through all the seasons of the past decade.

Some of these poems have been published in magazines and anthologies, including *Poetry Scotland, Northwords, Northwords Now, The Rialto, Island, Time Haiku, Earth Love, The Scottish Herald, Stramash, A Fresh Northerly and Snacks After Swimming.*

Introduction

'Cast' seems an appropriate verb for poets: more mystical than 'write,' and better than 'craft' or 'create' or 'make.' It captures an act of poetry as one of searching as well as one of construction: a hunt, angling to hook an unsuspecting reader with the contrivance of an artificial fly; a game of chance, albeit with a bit of knitting thrown in; words poured into moulds of metre and rhyme with a hope that they, like plaster on a broken bone, will help to heal what is hurt within. Like the shapes left in mud by worms, a poem is what is left, discarded rather than finished, after the process of writing comes to an end. And sometimes a poem emerging can feel like a shamanic act: when it goes well, it's a magic spell.

This collection has three parts:

The first part, Casting Ashore, is a collection of poems about my home: a wooded coastal croft in Achmelvich, Assynt, in the northwest Highlands of Scotland.

The second part, Casting Off, is a tribute to the River Kelvin in Glasgow.

The third part, Casting Adrift, consists of sightings and encounters from around the world.

Each of them is a product of inhabiting, of being a presence here, and of finding the words to stitch this moment into place.

Mandy Haggith
Assynt, Scotland
December 2006

Contents

Casting Off

Casting Adrift

Casting Ashore

Loch Roe Calm

Four seals loll on the skerry
contemplating four reflections.

Terns dance with their twins
kissing as they dip to fish.

Mirror-image dinghies
hang near siamese buoys.

A cloven yacht floats
masts and stays aligned into a diamond.

A breeze lifts
the diamond fractures
the doubles disintegrate.

Wind

The breeze presses the loch
persistently against the nearside rocks.
It's a mystery the far side does not run dry.
It's so funny, a gull is having hysterics.
Everyone is talking about it.
A curlew asks "Why?"
The heron rasps back "Because."
Outraged, an oyster catcher shrieks "!!"
"!!"
"!!"
To confirm its wizardry the wind
with one hand stirs the terns into a
white wheeling squealing cloud
and with the other
sweeps a sunbeam across the water.
Birch trees rustle in amazement.
Aspens flicker semaphore to the south shore woods
which respond with a Mexican wave.
A froth of seashore grassheads bob and dance like
    cheerleaders.
The loch is buzzing with conversation.
There is whispering behind the gleaming seaweed
    curtains.
Even the skerry seals are muttering.
Perhaps the nodding dinghy
will let me in on the secret.

Foam

all washed up
after a wild night
Guinness froth
on a seaweed moustache

Flotsam

When they brought the structures into the loch
they were not meant to stay here long
but no-one knew quite what to do with them –
old bits of fish farm cages, raft, walkway, ring.

Once they'd weathered a few big storms,
rocked and bobbed at the end of their mooring,
people got used to seeing them here
even though they're ugly and don't belong,

like the rest of us, they've somehow blended in
and the year moves monthly on and on,
yet inside the ring the water is always calm.
Anchors corrode but still hold tight to the ground.

Loch Roe

dazzling lights on the loch
flottilas of mysteries crowd
into our harbour

a notebook
a tree branch
a blue plastic bottle
three white feathers

I surrender
defenceless against the loch's advances
its seduction

as effortless
as inevitable
as cloud

High Tide

a birch leaf floats upstream
  bent river-wracks face inland
    pressed forwards by clear blue tide
      leaning in against a wall of freshwater
        ripples lap rocky banks
          making little white whirls
          doodling

            the leaf stops
            spins
            a heron shifts
            wracks straighten

            breath held
            the river licks
            a wet seam
            across its lip

            the leaf slides
          begins to glide
        the river blurs backwards
      coughs out peat froth
    the sea is taking its hand away
  melting the water wall to motion
wracks genuflect to ocean

Low Water

As the tide drops
it becomes self-evident
that it will continue falling

forever

exposing more and more
mud, weeds, rocks
and what has been submarine

forever

will become shore
once more.

Out in the Open

this morning she waded in up to her belly button
lobsters biting the backs of her knees
winkles in her knickers
fish having sex in her sex

by noon she was posing reflected in sunshine
only her muddy feet in the water
bladderwrack dress clinging to rocky limbs
underwear a squirm of slaters and stranded
    shrimps
knees crusty with barnacles
and that tell-tale white jelly stain on her skirt

now she's inching back in, letting it lap up her legs
nudging a hundred heads, a thousand tongues
under her petticoats
letting the tribe of tentacles touch her
slapping as they come into her
splashing as she plunges to meet them

Wishing Bone Poem

This is my story.
I am married to this peaty pool.
He washes me
quenches my thirst
is fond of amphibians and ferns
sparkles in breezes.
I show him my love
swimming in him
gently.

Earlier this summer
the arsonist sun
scorched him away.
I lay in the dry hollow
waiting for rain.
Storms came
but their waters drained away.
I wept in the dry hollow.
Salt tears crusted my face.

I went looking for my husband-pool
trawled the glens and mires
calling.
I found him in a dark rocky hole.
He bathed my eyes clear.
Ever since I have been bringing him home
little by little
cupped in my hands.

Gneiss Giantess

Birthed into a one billion year-old world,
Braighlinne was made of the earth's best gems
kneaded into metamorphic rock and baked.
This giantess, three billion years ago, stone born,
lay naked, breezes scuffling on resilient skin,
blithe dry until oceans condensed out of the sky.

Then floods and lochs and ground-down mountains
drowned her; crushed, incarcerated under silt
piling up high above her, hardening over,
cemented in a tomb, silenced, blinded,
Braighlinne writhed
squashed under seven miles of suffocating
    sandstone strata.

Wind, her first lover, saved her, stroked her,
scraped and whittled away at rock,
and with a heave she broke, calving a croft,
saw stars, settled. Her second inundation
was by sea, warm, erotic, teeming:
she let a crisp white body blanket her with lime.

Towards old age, she loved again, with ice
whose ravaging tore back the chalky sheets
laid her bare again, lithe, shapely, unconstrained.
In their rushing passion, the journeying glaciers
left erratic souvenirs of bouts with mountains:
carved quartzite boulders, porphyry trophies.

Now to the crone, skin lined with age and love,
trees have come, twisting toes in cracks, crushing
pebbles to grit, grinding gravels to loam.
Earth gives Braighlinne, the grey stone giantess,
her second, final metamorphosis
to wood, bud, leaf: gneiss crumbles into life.

A Song of Amergin

I am the wave that breathes upon the ocean
I am the ripple on the water
I am the flutter of aspen leaves
I am the hind of seven seasons
I am the raven on the rocks
I am a tear shed by the sun
I am honeysuckle
I am chanterelles
I am a badger in the woods
I am a salmon in the river
I am a lochan on the moor
I am a molecule of water
I am the twist in DNA
I am the point of the nuclear warhead
I am the custodian of madness
Who illuminates the summit on the mountain?
Who watches the tides?
Who will teach where the sun rests?

After a Week of Flat Calm

what relief to see the blades turn
to hear the rotor moan

housing to sou'west
gathering the best of the gusts

green lights flicker on enamel
ammeter jabs right, right, right

white tops on waves on Loch Roe –
force 7, good for a charge

Windy Night

the wind struggles
to unfasten
the moon-buttoned clouds

Storm Force Ten

a stadium of headbangers
roaring
to Storm Force 10

high up in the stand
one of the aspens
snaps

launches out
held up by the crowd
surfing the canopy

Kelvin Grove

Some legendary boat, nesting
behind this old shore dyke,
sheltered by this aspen grove,
left behind, like a golden egg,
this Kelvin engine, rusting.

Geese

Last spring when the geese flew over
I remember searching, searching,
unable to see them, their farewell cries
tugging like a feeling I could not identify.

Now I get them at the first whiff of a honk
and by the time the skein threads
over the horizon I'm there, marvelling
at the close, loose V-formation,
unravelling then zipping back up,

their hundred wings, my heart,
beating, carrying us away
to an arctic spring of floods and meltwater.

Sparrowhawk

He arrives at the office
wearing gloves,
holding a sparrowhawk,
his eyes child-round.

"She was trapped inside
splayed on the window."

So are you:
squashed up against the monitor,
flapping,
straining for him to open his hands.

Summer Smells of the Sea-flowers

honeysuckle is a geisha girl
sweeping her silk sleeve perfume
through the woods at dusk

waltzing with a sailor boy
a salt-scent swell who swings up from the shore
limber and strong

their dancing
a maritime schmaltz
tugs

                    clinches
                                    and twirls

Daydream

The lizard, ignored
basks, noticed
spirals into grass.
"What's wrong?"
Just a vanishing tail.

Bracken

no matter how much I cut you
your leaves unfurl again

like a child's hands held out
fist uncurling for gifts

a belt of sunshine
a lashing of rain

yellow flower blue flower

dandelion	knapweed
hawksbeard	clover
spearwort	woundwort
tormentil	thyme
bird's foot trefoil	devil's bit scabious
mouse ear hawkweed	cross-leaved heath
goldenrod	selfheal
cat's ear	foxglove
ragwort	milkwort
honeysuckle	ling

Chanterelles

tree-root-crowded earth buds
gold-leaf conspiracies

sphagnum-squashed twig-trapped
nut-butter truffles

finger-gentle cloud blooms
gifts from the invisibles

fruiting out of nothing
more than last year's memories

Autumn

rain is falling
    small soft pale drops
        stroking birches

leaves are drifting
    trembling yellow
        loose brown down

twigs are baring
    jewelled lattices
        open to air

trunks are lightening
    lichening
        tree boles sinking

roots are hiding
    deep strong fingers
        seeking stone

soil is growing
    living leaf-gold
        mouldering home

Dab Chicks

three little grebes
float among seaweed

like rubber ducks
in a laundry tub

they dive by vanishing
pop up like buoys

all grown up
still looking motherless

Dead of Winter

Gobbets of bloody fungus
spatter the track
through the woods.

Mosses leap out
silk scarves over velvet jackets
frisking passers-by.

A sleek pelt of dead leaves
sliced open
by bracken blades.

No culprit.
No motive.
Just a mystery.

Wood Sage

A wood sage sits quietly and green
unmoved by the snow
unruffled by the thaw
accepting our short day
without question
and the aspen nods
above it, in sleep,
perhaps in agreement,
or maybe to some inner hibernation music.

Famine

I can't sleep for the beseeching eyes
of the cow caught between loch and fence,
starving

her grey shaggy coat sodden with sleet
hocks muddied up to the thighs

meek, round, brown, that gaze
we know, that says
hungry

the slack fatigue of wasting flesh
the ground beneath her churned to a clag
the one birch sapling chewed to death

and us,
ripping weak wintry whisps of grass
from under trees, stuffing it through
holes in the wire

and the cow
munching with her mouth
her eyes still ravenous,
trapped.

Casting Off

Kelvin

gut of the city
gravy drain
duck domain

heron preening in a tree
neck telescoped in
pretend cormorant

gleaming blue magpie chuckles
a half-drowned tree imitates an otter
rabbits hop-dodge under brambles

hornbeams festooned with bunches of antlers
cowgirl tassels
trunks wet hide

a great tit teaches among brambles
'teacher, teacher, teacher'

rowanberries, haws
splatters of blood beside broken glass

people walk here too
among these rose-hips
like gobstoppers on sticks

holly leaves and a gum wrapper
shine in the winter sun

water reflecting sky

◆◆◆◆◆

... mud from the hills
blood of the city
leaves to the the sea ...

water like latte,
roast coffee brown
with whipped cream froth

Angel Delight before it is whisked stiff
churning under the blending current

gravy
flowing between forks of trees
banks bruised meat
with pastry crust bridges

◆◆◆◆◆

it smells fresh
fresher than soap
fresher than toothpaste
like fruit
a crisp apple
or a tangerine

◆◆◆◆◆

the woods
whose shadows can be trusted
        more than friends
whose leaves speak
        more quietly than words
        more reliably than promises

◆◆◆◆◆

like a lace blouse frothing out
from under a brown woollen sweater
the river spills over the V-necked weir

willows wait
one straddled corpse
struggles to stop the flow

below the weir the water boils
bubbling up like marmalade
not quite at the setting point
seething scum spreading out
in gushing spews

on the way back, thirsty
the river is a V-necked throat
water foams like beer down its gullet

♦♦♦♦♦

sticks, plastic bottles, a football
jostle by the bank
bumping and bouncing like children
daring the brown pound
drowning

popping up
downstream
hurrying back for more
spluttering as they come up for air

a stick jumps out of the water
a plank duck-
dives into the flow

a plastic cup waits among the willows
chicken

the plank comes back for more
thumps as it plunges
clears the water on the rebound
then is gone

♦♦♦♦♦

a heron studies still life on the far bank

♦♦♦♦♦

the rabid city river
spits froth

darts and switches
trapped between fields and sea

♦♦♦♦♦

not wanting to be streetwise
I am satisfied to know this river
that flows
    below banks
    under bridges
    through
this city I'll never belong to

Autumn River

deep
      green
            cold

alive with rotten scents
      of mushrooms
            truffles
                  and mould

fresh
      yet old

her diamanté motion
      seductive
            fecund
                  and bold

Kelvin River

willows trawl for sky
      above the weir
rain-stained beeches reflect

a mouse trickles under a leaf

dogs swirl in circles
      bumping
along the bank

their owners gush
and pause

a heron studies its   next   step

a magpie chuckles

the coot is
    content
    in the current

Duck

a mallard makes a V-line for bread
sporting a yellow plastic quack
on its green velvet head

After the Storm

Stranded logs have moved –
the trunk blocking the weir was freed by the flood

a wind-slaughtered tree is butchered where it fell
and a corpse that nearly got away gesticulates in the
    rapids
outraged at the meek acceptance of passers-by
and their oblivious dogs.

Looking at the River Kelvin

It is harder to walk
up river towards evening
than to follow it down into morning.

The blackbird is flying.
The river must be moving.

'Hush, hush' says the river
to the buses and cars
rushing across the bridge.

A Tesco trolley sleeps:
dreamy wheels turning
up the river aisle.

A thrush's solo
across the river
is all the song I need
to hear it's spring.

Passing the lofty church
the river goes white
and roars rugged roars
primal threats
to the silent stones.

green river running
fast fast
faster than the hour
faster than the year

... and when I see the river
I think of you
my love ...

What do a window frame, a fallen tree,
an Irn Bru bottle and a football
have to say to one another?
Why did the river gather them here today?

The goosanders are missing
but the river heron never misses anything.

One round inexplicable river ripple
for the willow to reflect on.

Cold fires burn under night water.
Stained glass river
I shall follow your hearths
to the Sargasso Sea.

I come down from the hills
like river-carried silt
froth
do not settle
only passing through

Casting Adrift

Night-walking

At dusk I stand, let footsteps fade, light dim,
listen to a wild boar huff, detect, move off.
The river chatters to the right. I look left
into the mystery of forest calm,

watch shapes loom up among the shadows, stare.
I let them scare me: ghostly mythic giant
silhouettes against the star-glow sky.
Each tree hides a secret shape of bear.

In willow scrub a musk of carnivore,
a scent voice: *I am watching, I am here.*
Passing pelts brush heady meadow hay.
Behind me silent paws pad on, away.

I don't need it easy, finding should be rare;
you, this, night-walking: my form of prayer.

Night Driving

black fabric unrolls ahead
tacked down with white stitches

one hand on the wheel
I pedal the machine

following the line
hemming 60 miles an hour

Airport

inside the glassy cadaver
we seeth
a bored unboarded swarm

wriggling in ticketed lines
squirming
between cavities of chrome

jet-fueled dragonflights hatch
breathe fire
lift metallic from the carcase

others circle
settle
gangway probosces suck

terminal flesh
bellies spawn egg-sack baggage
bundled into the bowels

pheremone logos
putrid with global slogans
send us scuttling

to sup and spend
grubs in a corporate body
waiting to depart

Forests

Some are dark hearts full of secrets of enslavement
some dry and dangerous
some alternately fly-infested and freezing
some damp and frail
but all spirit-rich
homes to folk with leaves in their eyes
(and mushrooms in their pockets)
who dream of chasing animals among branching
    shadows,
for whom the future is a tree-root that presses open
    rocks of the past,
with whom all stems intertwine,
in whom all saps and bloods and rivers mingle,
under whose power a single bud
becomes an eye, a wing, a soul,
becomes the whole
breathing planet.

Dawn

In Zimbabwe dawn strides in
with the confidence of Dali
deftly brushing the Zambezi escarpment
pink, azure and gold
to a fanfare of hippopotamus.

I'm more used to a swithering dawn
who tentatively shuffles in
with a pencil
to spend a few hours sketching Suilven
quietly, with a willow warbler.

Elephants

Six elephants cross the track
melt into mopane trees
shredding them
with a just-audible rustle
a delicate decimation.

Breakfast Bars

The sun squirms
through horizon-hugging cloud bars
announcing morning.

Lizardlike we bask on a log
letting the dawn chill thaw
blithely munching Bokomo breakfast bars.

There is a growling in the trees.
Leaving, we see a buffalo cow and calf
blithely munching dessicated jesse bush.

Suddenly the forest edge
is a rank of horned heads
bristling like a viking longboat.

Forty pairs of well-armed warrior eyes
(one hundred and sixty silent hooves)
are trained upon us.

We stride confidently away
(four wobbly legs)
joking at a safe distance about breakfast bars.

Senegal

this land is all beach
all portraits roasting under trees
a tilted man beneath a baobab
a washed-up foreigner basting beside a filao

donkeys line up nose to tail
in the shrinking slice of shade
beside the mosque at noon
smiling at a child's gift of peanut hay

but the beach lacks sea
fire its only element, no earth, no air, no water
only waves of sunshine, wind licking flames
    through trees
and scorched ground, dusty, dusty and dry

Tapkan

Gathered by trees to
brew in their cauldrons
of whispering leaves
then cast,

Tapkan raindrops spread
double-edged ripple-circles,
sometimes leaving a bubble
in the centre.

The water is so calm
within the round expansion
of a Tapkan ripple
a fish might dart by

or a small dead twig may
sprout head and legs
and creep about
preparing to fly.

Birds

birds ask questions
by the trickling stream

incomprehensible in the cool shade
inaudible in the deafening hot sun

time stops
by the trickling stream

Yichang

in from the riverside
where the putter of boat engines dulls

you practice scales
by a low pool among trees

long slow notes climb up your flute
as rain drops ring

young sad notes
almost as still as the leaves

sweet green notes
tugging at the sleeves of ghosts

pulling over the water
like a kind of grieving

reeling us in
to stand in the rain

listening

Yangtse Gorges

creepers dribble down the cliff's chin
from the mouth of its cave

monkeys sit on cliff ledges
hairy little buddhas
contemplating waterfalls

tilted strata remember an earlier horizon

Below the Floodline

below the floodline
cherry blossoms
will drown

the patchwork of green
yellow brown
will drown

roofless crumbling houses
already abandoned
will drown

caves
eyes in the valley wall
all will drown

dun grass, tangled shrubs
bamboo
will drown

ledges of
squabbling monkeys
will drown

the cracked fissured
disintegrating cliff
will drown

the water is milky
almost turquoise

graves
will drown

Trans-Manchurian

stopped
in a steppe siding
somewhere near the border
timetabled to be
impossible to be
late – drink another cup of tea
unspoken thoughts evaporate

pages of many lives exposed
Chinese, Russian, English
words in other tongues
lifting sleepily in wisps
mingling with samovar smoke and vapour
puffing from a frozen door
momentarily open

many readers too
breathe in between the lines
little understanding
voices babbling in the corridor
chatter over cards
stopped

in a steppe siding
somewhere near the border

Trans-Siberian

A full orchestra percussion section belts out from the bogies, a regular rumble of tympanum, cymbals, snare drum, bass drum, gong.

And a squeeze-box squeaks as we bounce, rocking us gently along.

The door opens onto the gap between carriages, the band hits sforzando; it closes bang and they're mezzo-piano again; while somewhere up in the corridor roof there's a woman's voice singing a familiar song.

Out there is a tartan sky, telegraph weft woven with silver birch grey and scruffy fields of sun-drenched snow seen through sparkling ice on the crusted window; it's a late winter day on the line and it's beautiful and long.

Taiga

the heavy-eyed forest purrs
yawns

its pelt burns
embers of the year's fire

amber leaves
sunbeam memories

smoke mist curls
exhaling summer fragrances

berry eyes close
a tiger flag of peace unfurls

Russian Snapshots

Autumn
After a summer of leaf dancing
the forest blushes maple red
undressing for winter

Anton
a bear raids a hunters' camp
feasts on kasha and watermelon
is punished with a chain
and a name

Banya
naked together in dark steam
banya master rustles leaves
flesh melts under oak-scent pelting

barefoot fire-sprung on the earth
ice-splash clean in moonlight
reborn into the taiga

Vodka
bottle cracks open
a clinking outburst of toasts –
the scorch of friendship

Poaching

a tree crashes to the littered floor
a chainsaw chews out a chunk

one more mouthful

to toss into the feeding frenzy
of Russian and Chinese timber sharks

Polar Bear

Low-angled sun gleams
through claret leaves
and caribou lichens pale green
in the first skiff of snow.

A frozen hare watches
the flight of a falcon
and spruce fingers point
where the winds will blow.

Tamarack needles flutter
and flurries of snow buntings dart
over flaming jade, bronze
and copper-leaved willow.

Photographers get set to lie
to freeze-frame your world
starched, ice-bleached arctic
whitewashing your rainbow.

Here you lie in the forest
a snoozing sumo wrestler
under trees barely able to hold
up the sky, so heavy with snow.

Pisew Falls

the lynx's mew is
drowned out
by the roar

crouching in the torrent
camouflaged
by hoar

hiding
in the freezing breath
of the falls

waiting to pounce
revealed
by claws

spilling off the smooth stone
pads
of her paws

Wealth

an Outspan Valencian orange
grown in South Africa
bought in Siberia
eaten in China

globalisation: so sweet, so juicy, so far

Nong Khai, Thailand

each leaf on every tree
a prayer

that need not be
spoken or heard or answered

but is
by wind or bird or butterfly

Sumatra

Yesterday I rode an elephant.
Today I swim.
Tomorrow I shall fly.

NOTES

Kelvin Grove: On my croft there is a sheltered place to pull boats up onto the shore. Here, long ago, a crofter-fisherman abandoned an old two-cylinder Kelvin boat engine. The shelter is provided by a grove of aspen trees, and so we jokingly refer to it as Kelvin Grove, an area of Glasgow to which it bears very little resemblance.

Wishing Bone Poem: This comes from a Cree story cycle: 'The Wishing Bone Cycle' by Jacob Nibenegenesabe.

Song of Amergin: Inspired by the ancient Irish poem of the same name, see Technicians of the Sacred, ed. Jerome Rothenberg, University of California Press, 1985, p341.

Tupkan: a Nepali word for raindrops that fall from the leaf of a tree.

Yichang: a town in central China, on the River Yangtse.

Below the Floodline: Due to the construction of the world's biggest hydro-electric dam, the level of the Yangtse is due to rise by 175 metres by 2009. Chongqing's monthly magazine, the Chongqing Current, describes the dam, apparently without irony, as "the greatest success of planning in China, successfully submerging 129 towns and relocating 1.3 million people." With successes like these, who needs natural disasters?

Trans-Siberian: The train line that runs between Moscow and Vladivostok, through Siberia, Russia.

Trans-Manchurian: The train line that runs between Irkutsk, Russia; and Beijing, China, through the northern Chinese region Manchuria.

Taiga: The Russian word (and more widely adopted ecological term) for the conifer-dominated forests of the boreal region, also known as snow forests or the forests of the northern lights. Between Russia (which has more forest than any other country), Canada and Scandinavia, and not forgetting Scotland's Caledonian forest fragments, taiga constitutes more than half of the world's forests.

Recent Titles from Two Ravens Press

Titles Published in April 2007

Love Letters from my Death-bed.
Cynthia Rogerson
The adventures of a Scottish bigamist dying – or is she? – in California. There's something very strange going on in Fairfax. Joe Johnson is on the hunt for dying people while his wife stares into space and flies land on her nose; the Snelling kids fester in a hippie backwater and pretend that they haven't just killed their grandfather; and Morag, multi-bigamist from the Scottish Highlands, makes some rash decisions when diagnosed with terminal cancer by Manuel – who may or may not be a doctor. Meanwhile, the ghost of Consuela threads her way through all the stories, oblivious to the ever-watching Connie – who sees everything from the attic of the Gentle Valleys Hospice.
£8.99; ISBN 978-1-906120-00-9

Highland Views. David Ross
Military jets exercise over Loch Eye as a seer struggles to remember the content of his vision; the honeymoon is over for workers down at the Nigg yard, and an English incomer leads the fight for independence both for Scotland and for herself … This debut collection of short stories from a gifted writer provides an original perspective on the Highlands, subtly addressing the unique combination of old and new influences that operate in the region today.
£7.99; ISBN 978-1-906120-05-4

Castings. Mandy Haggith

A collection of poems by Mandy Haggith, whose writing clearly reflects her love for the land and her concern for the environment – not just in the North-West Highlands where now she lives on a woodland croft, but in her travels around the world.
£8.99; ISBN 978-1-906120-01-6

Riptide: New Writing from the Highlands and Islands. Edited by Sharon Blackie and David Knowles

A collection of microfiction, short stories and poetry by writers from the Highlands and Islands – established writers and names to watch. Includes contributions by Andrew Greig, Cynthia Rogerson, John Glenday, Angus Dunn and many others.
£8.99; ISBN 978-1-906120-02-3

Titles Forthcoming in July 2007

Types of Everlasting Rest: a collection of short stories from Scotsman-Orange Prize Winner and novelist Clio Gray
£7.99; ISBN 978-1-906120-04-7
The Language of It: a poetry collection by Stephen Watts
£8.99; ISBN 978-1-906120-03-0

Titles are available direct from the publisher at
www.tworavenspress.com, or from any good bookshop.

Two Ravens Press Ltd., Green Willow Croft, Rhiroy, Lochbroom, Ullapool IV23 2SF. Tel. 01854 655307